Closets and EnSuites Design

BEDROOM DESIGN

Brian Rider

CLOSET & ENSUITE

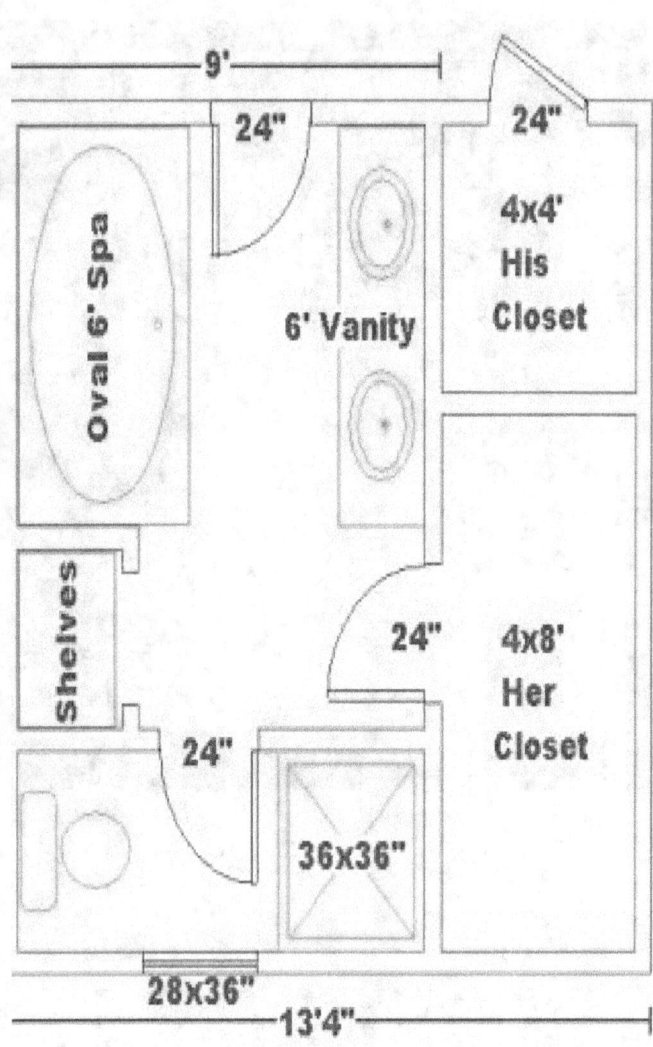

9'

24"

24"

4x4'
His
Closet

Oval 6' Spa

6' Vanity

Shelves

24"

4x8'
Her
Closet

24"

36x36"

28x36"

13'4"

01

DESIGNING AN EN SUITE IS A COMMON REQUEST BUT BECAUSE OF THE PLUMBING YOU NEED TO PLAN WISELY - THE BUDGET CAN BECOME A RUNAWAY

EnSuite

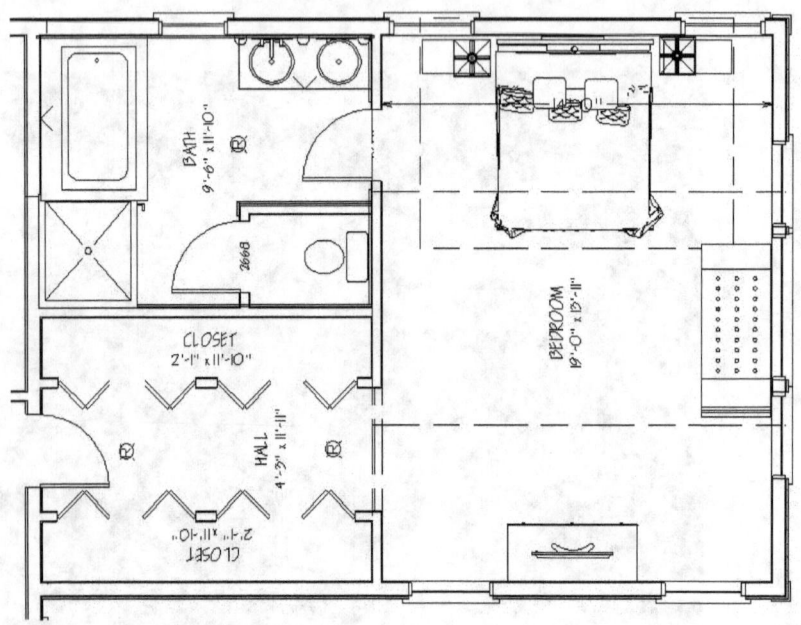

An efficient layout with all the necessary features but why the separate w.c.? A modesty panel would have served the same purpose and allow handwashing without contaminating the door handle. Why make the bath deeper than the shower?

Why walk through the closet to get to the en suite and bedroom?

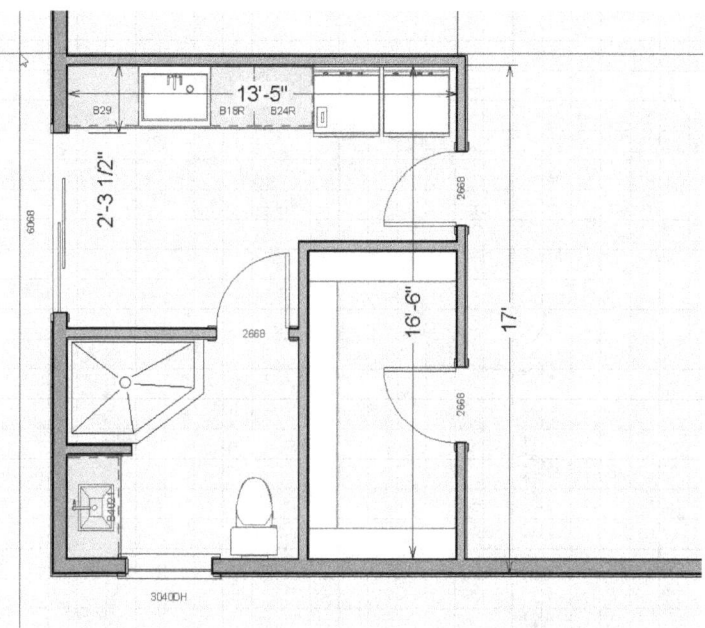

The bedroom is to the right in this plan. Small walk in closet but perfectly adequate. A dressing room with washbasin and a lot of space - probably too much space. Nice en suite but perhaps the toilet swapped with the basin would make a big improvement in utilised space.

Presumably the sliding doors shown in the dressing room area open to a balcony. I would have been inclined to make access to the closet from the dressing room to leave the bedroom wall uncluttered. And probably swap the toilet and shower, plumbing permitting, borrowing a little space from the closet and using a quadrant not the pentangle.

Perhaps adding a small shower to the RH of the dressing room and an extra wall hung w.c. in the dressing room.

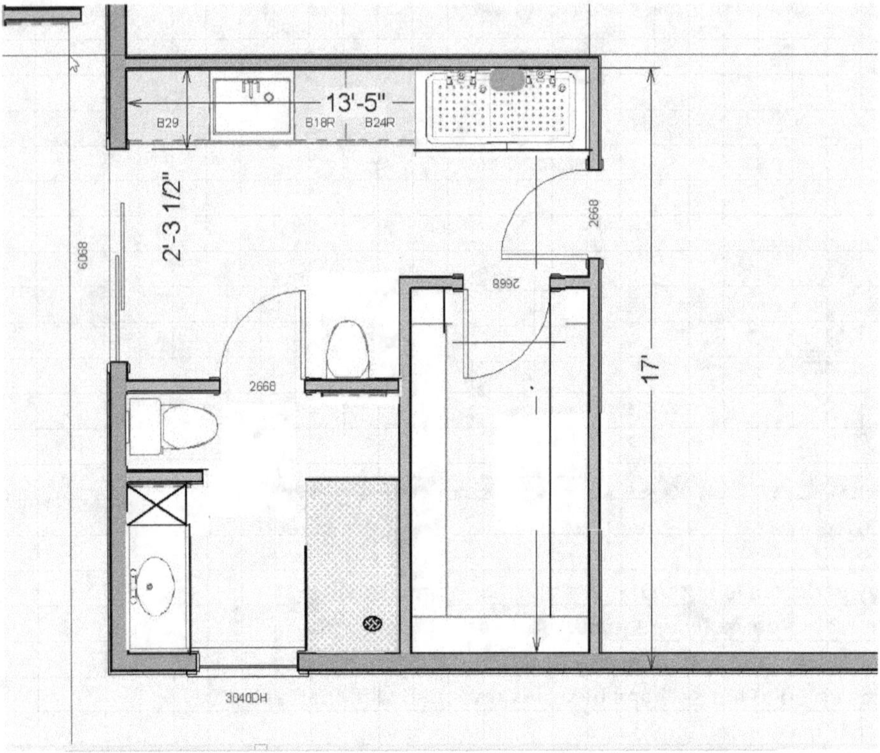

13'-5"

B29   B18R   B24R

2'-3 1/2"

6068

2668

2668

17'

2668

3040DH

Suggested additional changes. Possibly move the wall between the sliding doors to balcony allowing a little more space for the toilet. Apart from moving the closet door we have not altered the actual room and used a walk in shower in the main en suite. But moving the closet door to one side or the other would enable deeper storage area on one side only?

MEDIA AREA

02 | A lot of people use a computer in their bedroom complex. Virtually everyone these days has music and video entertainment in the room.

This layout could easily be adapted for a large bedroom dressing room.

This is a really comfortable and elegant layout but possibly not ideal for a computer

Add a computer and wireless keyboard and you have an excellent set up

This is fairly simple to include in a modestly large bedroom and would accommodate the computer section easily.

A bit heavy but has all the requirements

This is essentially similar to the previous unit but has a heavier feel for more formal furniture.

Another imposing layout but in a nice light presentation

This one could easily be a part of the bedroom proper and could be adapted for storage as well as decorative use.

My favourite layout. Add a mac mini, wireless keyboard
and mouse, connect to the right hand screen and you have
a system for everyone. Could also be used with a tablet or
laptop.

GOOD BEDROOM DESIGN

03 | There seem to be very few bedroom planning design guides and yet it is one of the most important rooms in the house.

efficient and yet attractive use of the features available in your product range

innovative use of the features

style in keeping with the property

style in keeping with the buyer's lifestyle

DRESSING TABLES

DRESSING TABLE THOUGHTS

- large mirror
- multi view mirrors
- natural lighting
- also good overall lighting
- theatre style lighting?
- storage for jewellery
- makeup
- diary
- tablet>
- electrics
- chair not stool

04

The example shown above has an inadequate mirror and no sign of lighting?

Mirror ok but no lighting.

Computer is bigger than the mirror? Again no lighting

BEDSIDE CABINETS & FEATURES

05

In classic bedroom design the overbed and niche display is usually the one that makes the sale.

Nice display but No electrics?

BEDSIDE THOUGHTS

- Display
- lighting
- electrics for charging stations
- perhaps a charging dock
- shelving and \or niche
- drawer space
- intimate items
- medicines
- headphones for tablet and TV jack

This has a nice display design but the bedside lamps are clumsy and very distracting. Surely they could have designed something a bit more attractive. Or maybe it was just the dumb householder realising that they should have some lighting, so added it after?

However, with the lighting improved, the layout is excellent

Classic design with a bit of breakfronting and good lighting and electrics.   Probably good enough for most buyers on a budget.

This is probably the basic style in any bedroom planners kit bag. Looks good works well.

Stunning and boring at the same time. Nice pull out tables which would be very useful in a different setting where space is at a premium. I assume this is a fold up bed a la James Bond. Great for attic conversions.

Pretty in Pink.

Obviously a teen bedroom which, strictly speaking, we are not covering here but the decor is stunning.

Classy arrangement which seems to answer the minimalist urges.

Lighting is adequate but not great.

Neat, tidy and efficient and definitely saleable.

Just a little worried about the drawers but I am assuming it is just the drawer fronts that are angled and the drawer box pulls out straight.

26

They are obviously going to spend a lot of time in this gorgeous bedroom but may need sunglasses.

I sincerely hope they are using energy efficient lamps. Especially in the downlighters as these are often not great lasters.

Very pretty. who is going to clean that mobile?

There was a bit of a fetish with lighting features in the noughties but this one is probably the worst I have seen. The ladyof the house is likely to be fusier in the bedroom than anywhere else in the house. Imagine all the dust cascading from the mobile while wielding your feather duster.

Very interesting arrangement and obviously fully comprehensive although the lighting is a little suspect.

This layout needs quite a bit of space to pull it off but it is an extremely interesting layout. I only wonder what the slightly taller unit is the lthe left of the bed. Almost looks like a morning tea cabinet.

06 EN SUITE- EASY CLEAN OR WHAT?

Let's have a look at our first planning consideration

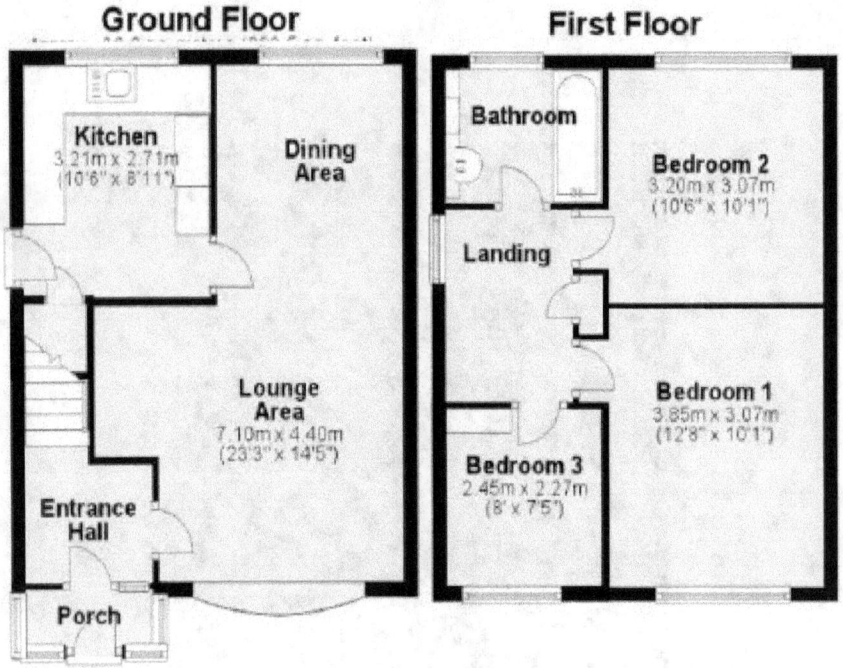

Ground Floor

Kitchen
3.21m x 2.71m
(10'6" x 8'11")

Dining Area

Lounge Area
7.10m x 4.40m
(23'3" x 14'5")

Entrance Hall

Porch

First Floor

Bathroom

Landing

Bedroom 2
3.20m x 3.07m
(10'6" x 10'1")

Bedroom 1
3.85m x 3.07m
(12'8" x 10'1")

Bedroom 3
2.45m x 2.27m
(8' x 7'5")

Where do we begin. One possibility is that the customer already has a floor plan of the house. Any house built within the last 20 years probably has one and most estate agents working online will supply one.

Planning Thoughts

Looking at our house plan, Bedroom 1 is the master bedroom and logically we would like to use bedroom 3 for the en suite but there is no easy waste access. the customer only needs 2 bedrooms so I would be inclined to suggest leaving bedroom 3 and using bedrooms 1 and 2 for the master and en suite which leaves the existing bathroom for exclusive use by bedroom 3.

Obviously we will need to have a door between bed 1 and bed 2 and seal the existing door of bedroom 2. this would leave us a very large en suite so we will make the first part of the new ensuite into a dressing, closet and showerroom. Probably the best division would be in line wit the existing wall of the bathroom giving us a nice dressing/closet area and a reasonable size ensuite. There isn't enough space either side of the window so we will use the right hand side for a large quadrant curving towards the window. The w.c. and basin area would be backing on to the existing bathroom and we would also install another basin on the left hand side of the dressing area with the closet to the right.

 Alternative closet arrangement with reworked entrance door. In both cases the dooor/arch to the bathroom area may need repositioning.

Vanity Area

Alternative vanity and closet area with false window.

First Floor

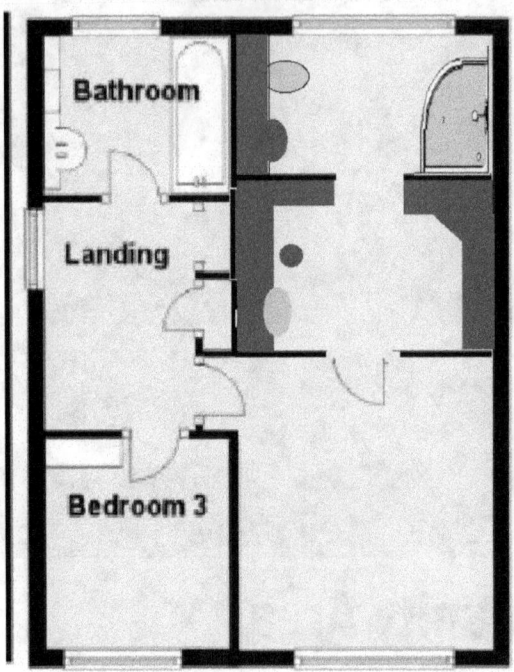

This is a possible plan for the en suite area using a vanity pack with btw wc and concealed cistern. The furniture effectively hides any plumbing work which will connect with the existing bathroom plus conceal the extension for the basin in the dressing area.

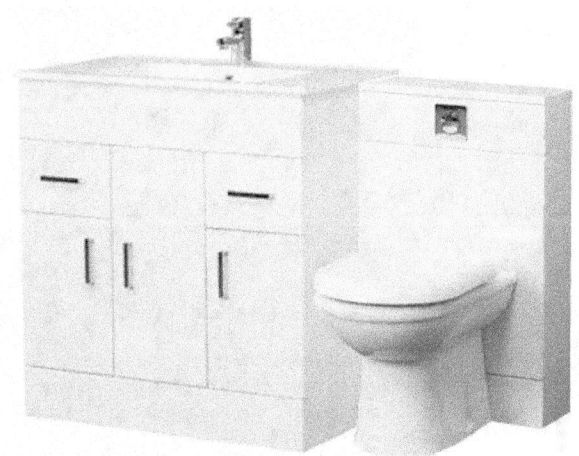

DRESSING ROOMS

07

This is a project that should interest any owners of reasonable sized property possibly where the kids have left home to enjoy their adult lives and maybe find a few spare bedrooms about. A dressing room with the ensuite and if possible a modern walk in closet and even his and hers.

1. Plenty of storage for all requirements

2. often referred to as a closet or walk in closet but there should be a distinction

3. should be adjacent to the en suite

4. ideally his 'n hers

WHAT IS A DRESSING ROOM?

It doesn't have to be large but it should be big enough to incorporate a dressing table with a generous size mirror and good overall lighting plus a full length mirror able to easily see the view from behind and probably, ideally a chevalier mirror.

In the grander households it could be possible to have a his 'n hers dressing room and en suite for really comprehensive facilities. The his group can be smaller and would only need a shower.

Excellent Dressing
Room and Closet

This has almost everything but the kitchen sink. Or should I say vanity sink. Such a pity that they didn't finish it off properly. You could easily accommodate a sink in the worktop under the window

Lavish Traditional Dressing Room and Closet

A bit elaborate for me but it does have everything although a nicely upholstered chair might have been better than the stool?

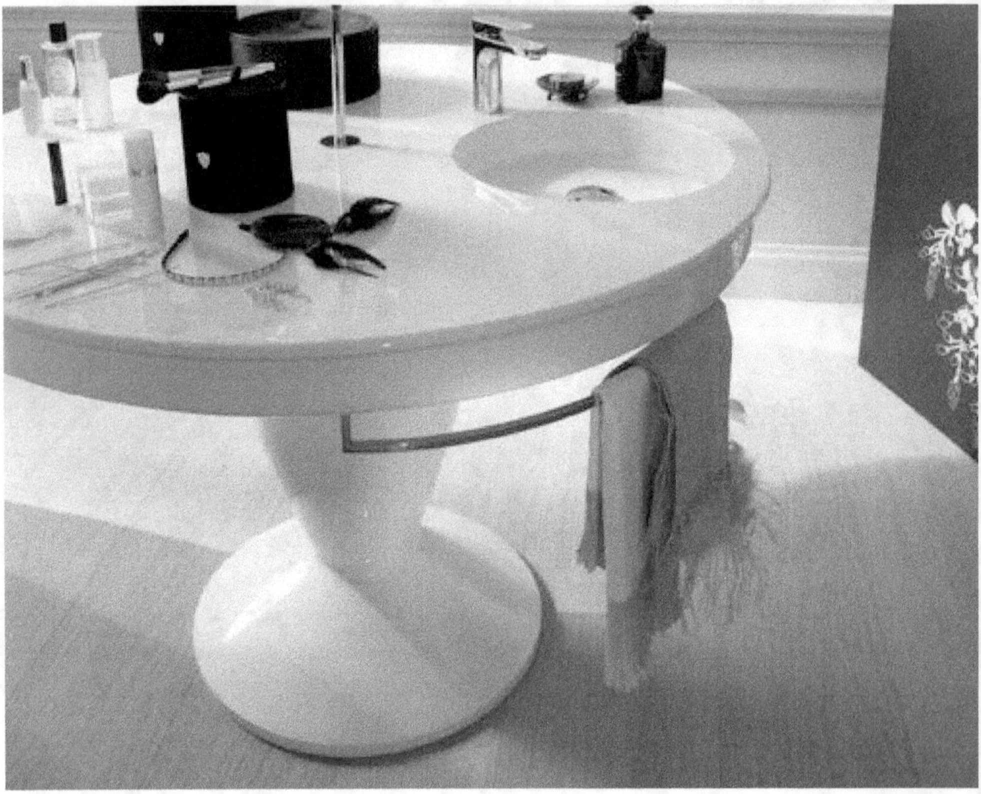

Modular Vanity for
Dressing Room

This is a great take on a vanity basin for a dressing room and I can see this as a big attraction in any en suite dressing room situation. Obviously it needs a waste but in a big en suite and bedroom revamp shouldn't be a problem

CLOSETS

08 | This American term is slightly misunderstood. in Modern parlance a closet is really a walk in closet which will usually combine some functions of a dressing room.,but essentially is a storage for clothing. Ideally a house would have his and hers.

Compact Closet

This layout is simple and compact and would form the basis of a dresser / closet perhaps for a young lady?

Closets do not have to be huge but clearly the compact unit above would probably require additional robe space.

HOUSE STUDIES

09

| Let's have a look at this largish house and see how we can develop the master bedroom into a full en suite, dressing room/closet arrangement.

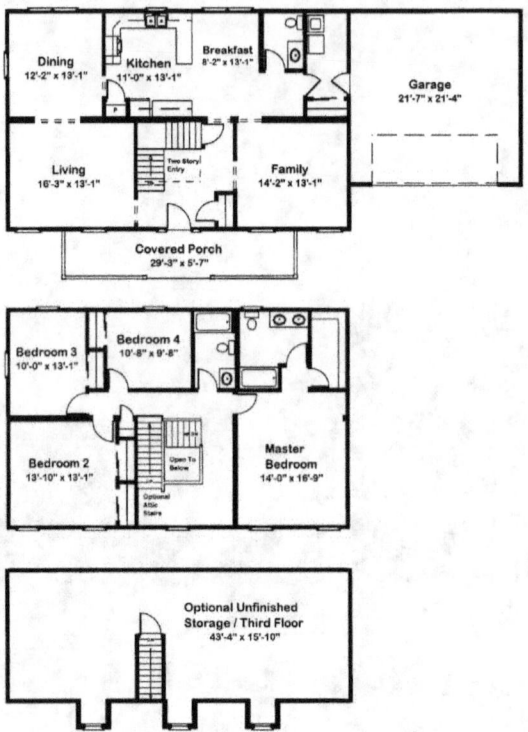

This is a fairly large property. For some reason or other they have left the third, top floor without and real planning. This then becomes our focus as it is a very promising area to develop.

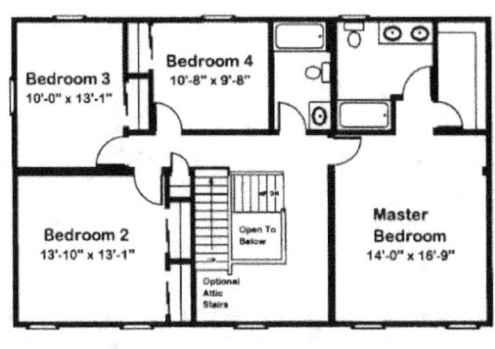

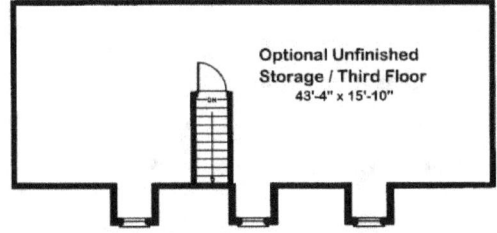

EXISTING BEDROOMS QUITE GOOD BUT NO DRESSING ROOMS

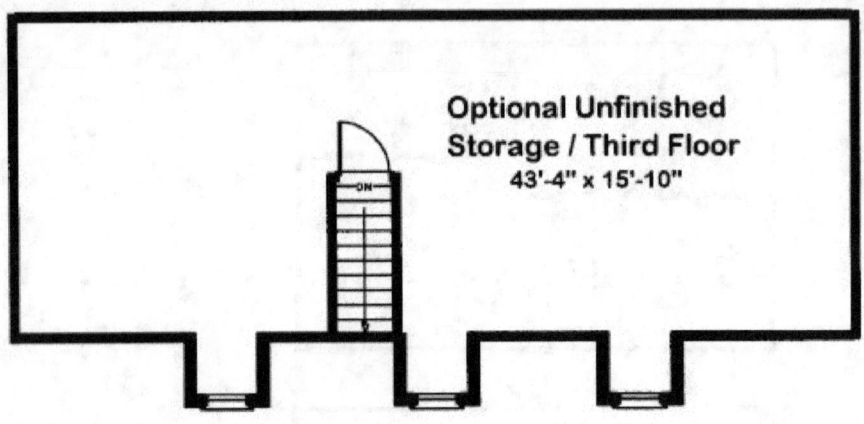

Optional Unfinished Storage / Third Floor
43'-4" x 15'-10"

PLENTY OF SPACE. How can we develop this.

Ignore the budget at the moment. Building vs content?

House not built yet

third floor could be developed

Stairs could be repositioned. Even a lift could be installed but an emergency staircase would be needed although this could go at the ends of the building.

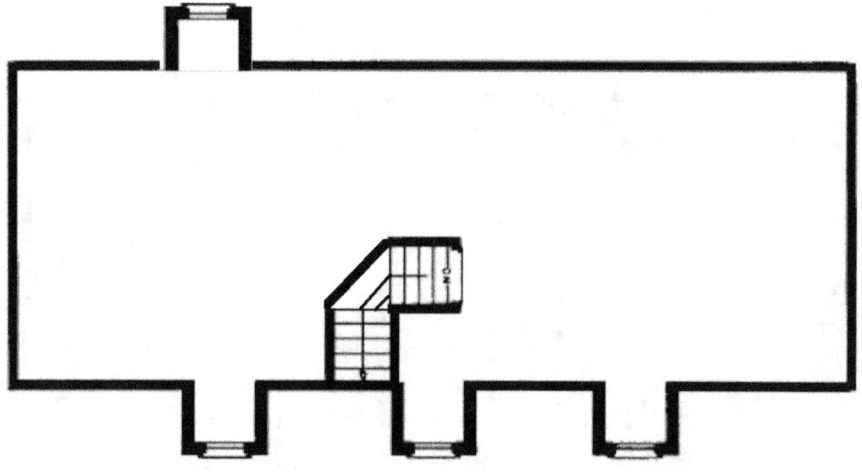

This is the top floor with an altered staircase to afford more
flexibility in the layout.

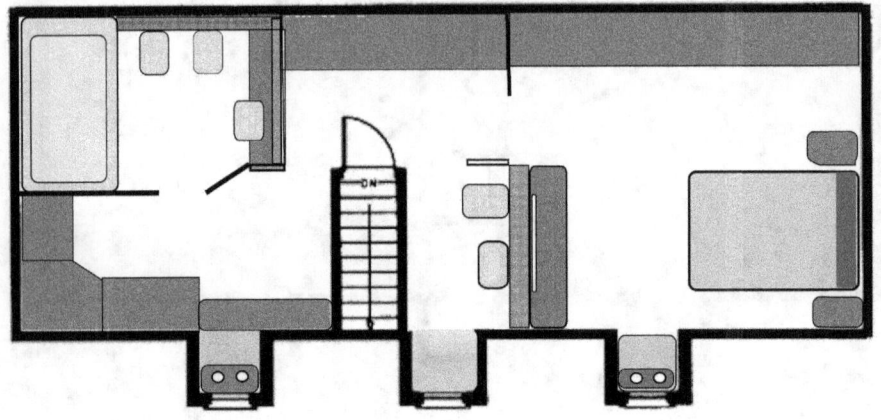

**Possible layout using the initial staircase and his and hers
en suites and dressing rooms**

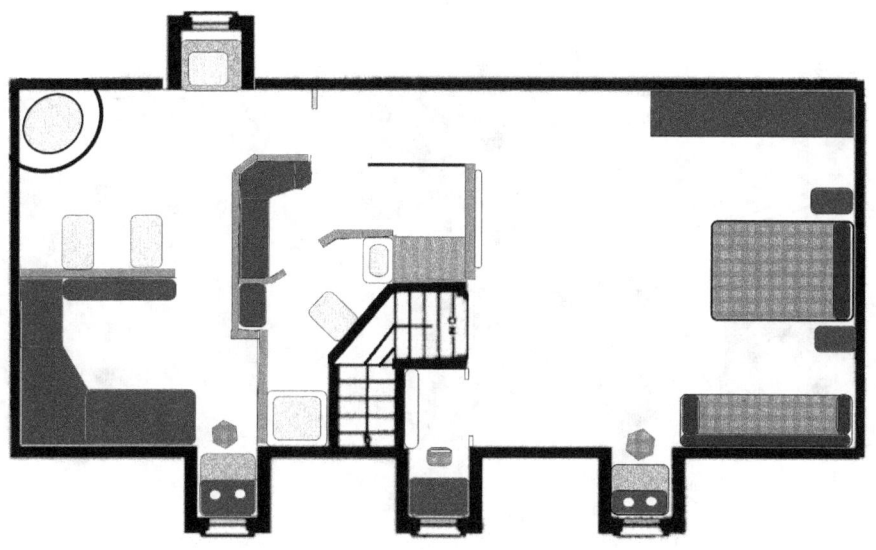

Another layout using the modified staircase and allowing a bit more imaginative setting again with his and hers facilities.

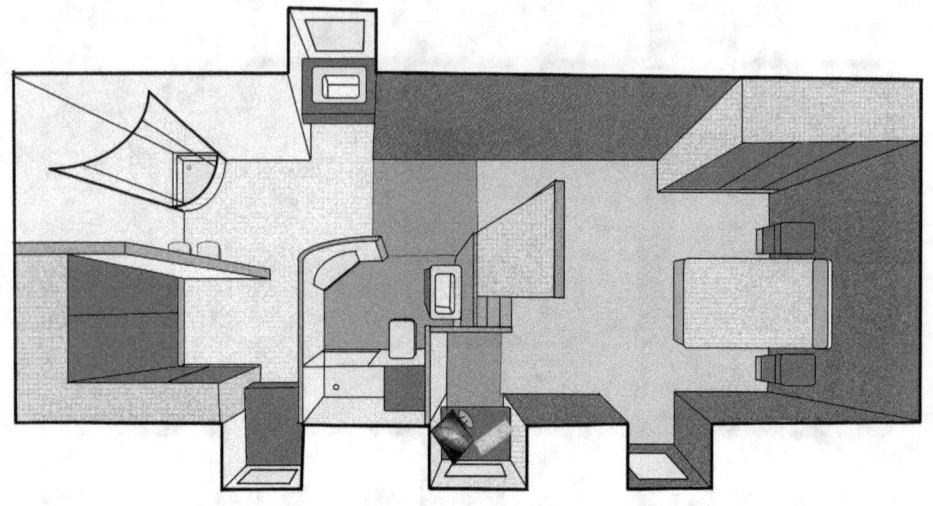

Bird's Eye presentation which is the best way to depict a large room. This is the cranked staircase. You can just see the stairs entering the bedroom but slightly hidden by the perspective of the tall closet.

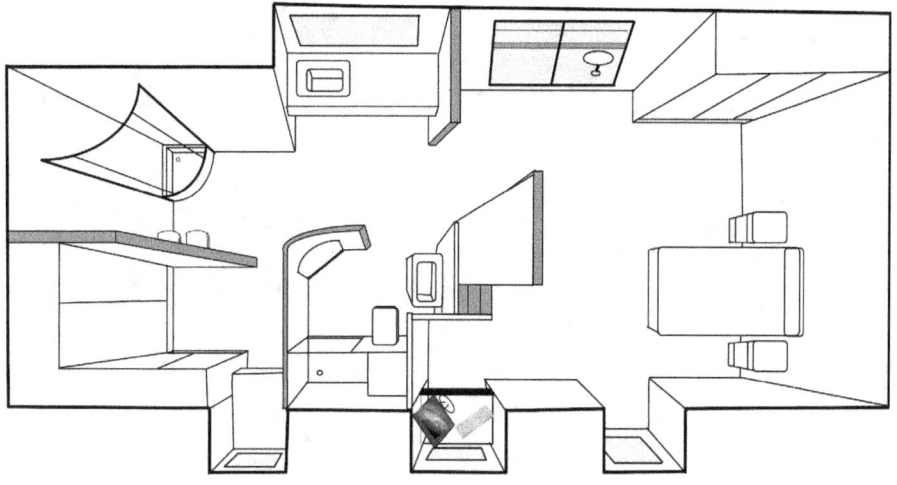

This is the ultimate design alllowing the room to be
extended rearward using the stepped window areas at the
back. Not a difficult concept as the roof would only need
slight modifcation.

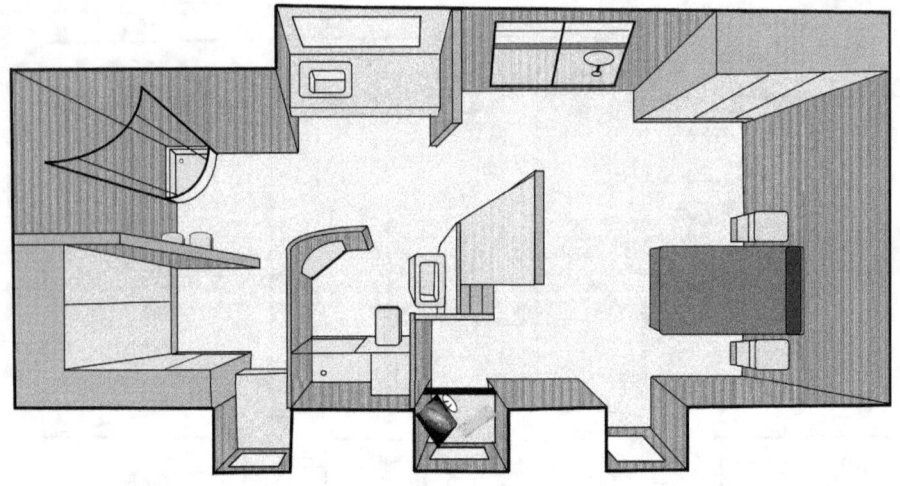

Bedroom furniture is freestanding so would be to customer's choice

a/v centre to spare wall adjacent to computer room niche

0
I

We have seen how the planning ideas can develop as you think through
the project and build possible layouts. Now its your turn.

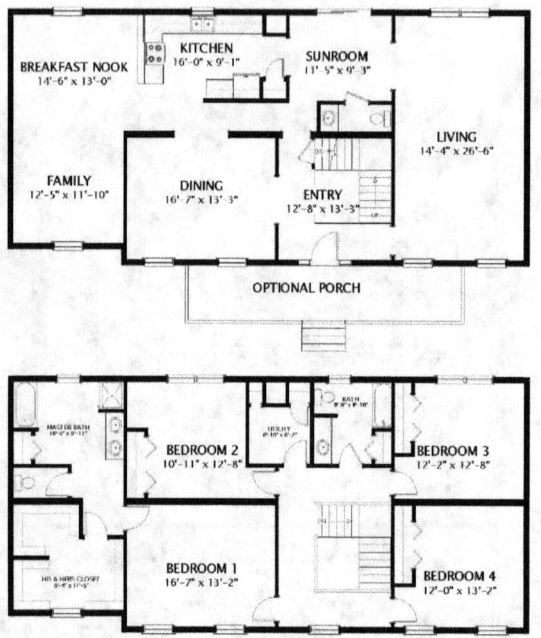

Floor plan of our house exercise. Quite well designed but could be better.

This is the bedroom floor. Your task is to redesign the layout to give an improved his and hers layout. the thinner walls are all internal and can be modified or removed. Only 3 bedrooms are needed.

Draw a Bird's Eye presentation. There is a mini guide for this discipline available at the bargain price.

Thank you for purchasing this latest version of our EnSuite and Closet mini guide

We want you to enjoy this publication and learn from it,

To this end we offer TOTAL SUPPORT - if you feel you need help or clarification on any points please log in to our website at

www.kbb2000.com

Some current mini guide titles - not all are on general release if in doubt enquire on the website

KITCHEN PLANNING ESSENTIALS

I POINT PERSPECTIVE & VANISHING POINT

KITCHEN PLANNING APPLIANCES ESSENTIALS

2 POINT PERSPECTIVE & VANISHING POINT

KITCHEN PLANING + DESIGN

BIRDS EYE PERSPECTIVE

BATHROOM PLANNING

BEDROOM PRESENTATION

BATHROOM DESIGN

BATHROOM PRESENTATION

Avery C32011

SURVEYING TECHNIQUES

EXTERIOR PRESENTATIONS

GRANNY FLATS

CLOAK ROOMS DRESSING ROOMS CLOSETS

KITCHEN WORKING TRIANGLE 2016

DOUBLE WORKING TRIANGLE

CAD VS BRAIN